Stovetop Ghosts
a book of hours

by Katy Naylor

Advance Praise for *Stovetop Ghosts*

"In *Stovetop Ghosts*, Katy Naylor captures the elusive presence we all search for in our day-to-day chaos. This collection of poetry is one you will wear out returning to for a glimpse. Whether you are in the thick of life with family and career, well past it, or haven't even started, this book of hours reads as a meditation on what is important in life. Those little things; the painful and the joyous, the frivolous and the critical are revealed through Katy's stunning language and surprising insights. Katy holds her words and world in front of her, so transparent you can see through them and into your own."
—Kellie Scott-Reed, AEIC, Roi Faineant Press

"Katy Naylor's *Stovetop Ghosts* prays with parents everywhere, but the collection isn't just for parents or followers of a certain faith. Naylor explores what it means to be human through this collection of poems, which are accompanied by artwork by Emma Levin. She sees all the perfect imperfections, the anxiety and the mindsets etched by words of others and how we are shaped as much by shattered mugs as by the warming sun. Katy's collection beams with an authentic voice and an authority on the topic, but the poems resonate and ripple outward allowing for deep and varied thought and interpretation. The collection sings with personality and life, lingering long after stoves are scrapped and ghosts are quiet."
—Matthew McGuirk, author of *Oil Stains Like Rorschachs*

"Katy Naylor's *Stovetop Ghosts* is a collection of prayers - the kind of prayers you tuck away in the corners of your house to keep the ghosts away and keep the firelight in. Domestic and ethereal, nostalgic yet immediate, these pieces resonate in their familiarity even as Naylor weaves words in ways uncanny and strange. Read as if in a dream and chase those shadows you'd like to keep as Naylor whispers in your ear – it's a fine way to spend an afternoon."
—Arden Hunter, EIC of *Cutbow Quarterly*

STOVETOP GHOSTS

a book of hours

KATY NAYLOR

Copyright © 2023 Katy Naylor

All Rights Reserved. This book or any portion thereof may not be reproduced, in whole or in part, in any form (beyond that permitted by Sections 107 and 108 of the U.S Copyright Law and except by reviewers for the public press) , without the express written permission of the publisher except for the use of brief quotations in a book review.

Naylor, Katy / author

Stovetop Ghosts / Katy Naylor

Poems

ISBN: 979-8-9869524-1-3

Edited by: Amanda McLeod
Book Design: Katy Naylor
Cover Art & Design: Emma Levin

PUBLISHER
Femme Salvé Books
An Imprint of Animal Heart Press
P.O. Box 322
Thetford Center, Vermont 05075
www.femmesalvebooks.net

Table of Contents

Introduction

I   Lauds

II   Matins

III   Terce

IV   Sext

V   Nones

VI   Vespers

VII   Compline

Introduction

The book of hours is a devotional text for everyday people. Popular in the middle ages, they were small, often lavishly decorated books that contained prayers and contemplative texts to be read throughout the day. They followed the patterns of prayer in monastic life, marking the hours of *lauds* (dawn), *matins* (early morning), *terce* (mid-morning), *sext* (noon), *nones* (mid-afternoon), *vespers* (dusk) and *compline* (nightfall).

This book is secular, but it is a book of hours all the same. I wrote it about time at home with small children, when the hours seem to bend and stretch unnaturally, and devotions of a different kind are required. In it, I aim to express the small triumphs and larger doubts, and the ghosts of past and future that linger over the hearth and cast a long shadow.

Each poem within this book of hours can be read as a prayer of sorts, called out above the ebb and flow of the day. I hope that within the cycles captured between its pages you can find something that speaks to you.

LAUDS

I.

aleidoscope hours.

Neon and sweat and bass.

Swapping stories and cigarettes as the dawn reaches out across the rooftops.

It's a slow fade,

the afterimage almost gone.

Your small hand is in mine:

a warm weight.

Your eyes, so slowly, start to close.

I sway as I make for the nursery door.

The old rhythm is still there; and an older rhythm still.

The shadows dance on the wall.

II.

rozen, I stare up at the surface of the water

try to make peace with the pleasant chill, the muddied light through the weeds

still my heart as I watch for heron-thin legs

the sharp beak that'll pluck me gasping into everyday air

MATINS

I.

y better self is clear as glass today.
She floats, bright, just beyond my fingertips.
The moment stretches meniscus thin:
I hold out my hand -

- a yell - you've dropped your favourite cup -
and I'm standing in the fragments.
She shimmers and is gone,
lost in a flurry of tea towels and tears.

I close my eyes, will her to come back
and for a moment I see all those tomorrows,
second chances winding silver into the distance,
if I could only reach a little further.

II.

 ot butter blisters.
Milk, eggs, flour spit fury from the pan.

They never turn out how I hope:
thick, misshapen, left too late;
raw, or stretched too thin.

My mother watches a remembered stove.
Floured arms, the scalding frown
I still feel hissing at my back.

A curl of smoke rises from the pan:
another drop of disappointment.
I can taste the taint.

You shriek in delight,

  anoint yours with a smear of jam.

Your joy a benediction

Maybe not all spirits have to share our table.

Maybe, sometimes, this is enough.

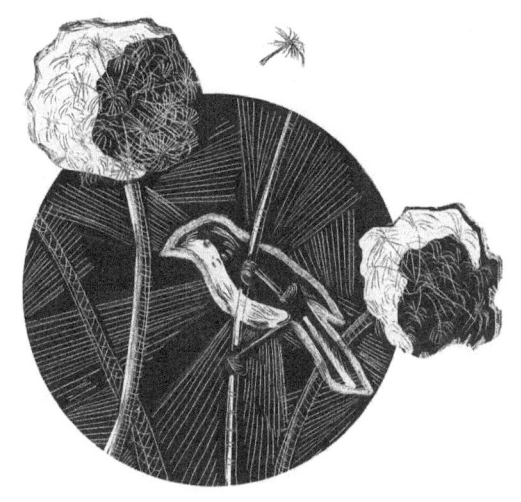

TERCE

I.

he burn in carpet, the red wine stain,
melted wax on the countertop, birthday-bright,
the trail of fingerprints smeared toddler-tall along the walls.

Plaster saints to receive our prayers:
only let it get better;
only let it stay like this.

Let these circles hold.
Let them ripple out,
flickering flames spreading before the dark.
Small, bright testaments to our imperfection.

II.

he devil is deep blue, and very cold.
His caress freezes.
Brush his arm, look him in the nebula-deep eye,
move a little further out into the waves.
Ice-fields and glaciers float ahead, sterile and endless.

The longing for the chill has never left me.
The empty drift, cauterised with ice.
The grey sky above the waves, blessed silence.

Only now there's you
by the fire on the shore.
You're building a small stack of pebbles.

You don't look up as I join you there -
you don't see me look back at the water.

A beacon doesn't know it's a beacon.
The sun doesn't feel the cracks left by the thaw

SEXT

he story goes
that when they spied the Kraken's head
sailors set off home-made flares
for the fleet on the horizon.

Legend has it
that when he had abandoned his barque
and the captain washed up on a lonely shore,
he lit beacons every night
for the shadows of passing ships.

Coffee, sandwich,
a buzz in his pocket.

I light my match -
my last pinch of dry powder -
I watch the waves for a sign.

NONES

I.

ubbles and suds

        (thrum thrum)

I could have flown

        (thrum thrum)

but here I sit

        (thrum thrum)

pinned and split

(thrum thrum)

tuned to the pitch

(thrum thrum)

and the churn of the drum

(thrum thrum)

II.

The time you take to walk down to the far end of the
allotments, where the blackberries grow
studying every stick and leaf
singing a song about knees.

The time you take to blow the dandelion clock,
fuzzed haloes
growing thinner with each puff.

I wish I could hold this bright drop of now;
that the afternoon didn't lie curled in the morning sun;
the bright green clean spring leaves didn't whisper autumn.

I think about those seeds
drifting on the wind to who knows where.
Green shoots and yellow flowers I'll never see.
Stems for little hands to hold and begin again.

VESPERS

I.

onday! Tuesday! Wednesday! Thursday!
You serenade your stew.

You are starting to anchor yourself in time -
you lace it through your fingers like a cat's cradle.

I am counterweight and shuttle, complicit.
Once those threads are woven there's no unravelling them.

In this moment the web still floats wide -
wide as your arms, flung out
as you wind the bobbin up and clap, clap, clap.

II.

ometimes I walk through the forest

on the very edge of dusk -

the air sharpening,

the branches' shadows lengthening -

and I could sing

for the pleasure of being here.

And I stare

into the mouth of the onrushing dark,

unhinging,

but it is not here yet.

It's not here yet.

COMPLINE

I.

 am my own cemetery, all buried down deep -
black glass canal ripe with echoes, a resounding chill.
I listen to the crows, focus on my feet,
waiting for the tremor in the earth,
the first grey fingers pushing up through the soil.

The stars above blink in code across aeons, bright and distant.
My message is slow growing, too.
These bulbs were planted years ago -
harsh words, rough hands waiting to bloom,
seeding growths I'll have to pull, years from now.

I shrink from my own eyes, unblinking among the stones,
willing myself to escape -
wake up tomorrow and see the snowdrops.

II.

 stare into the wide-awake dark,
headlights wheeling across the ceiling,

and I wonder if it's your voice I hear down here
or just an echo of my own.

The walls are narrow, slick,
the water rising with each pulse.

I look up, watch for a coin -
a wish, or to measure how far I've fallen.

I look up, watch for a rope -
a weight too much for little arms to bear.

I imagine the rise and fall of your breath,
peaceful as the moon
draped in soft squares over your body.

While you're here I can wait -
my gazed fixed on the small circle of light
just too high above.

Acknowledgments

Thank you to:

Emma Levin, for the beautiful cover art and illustrations.

Eli, Beth, and Amanda at Femme Salvé Books, for believing in this work and giving it a home.

Fevers of the Mind Poetry, for publishing 'Vespers (1) '
Not Deer Mag, for publishing 'Vespers (2) ', and 'Compline (2) '
Selcouth Station, for publishing 'Prime (1) '
Resurrection Mag, for publishing 'Sext'

Dave, for his constant support and encouragement (and understanding when the perfect idea comes at 2am) .

My Mum, Val, and my children, for being the source and anchor to all of this.

About the Author

Katy Naylor lives by the sea, in a little town on the south coast of England. She writes in the time that falls between the cracks. *Stovetop Ghosts* is Katy's third published chapbook, and one that contains much of her heart. Be gentle with it.

www.ingramcontent.com/pod-product-compliance
Lightning Source LLC
Chambersburg PA
CBHW032105040426
42449CB00007B/1189